To Jon —
— with our complete
respect and admiration —
Thanks for showing us a
living example of the
ideals expressed in this book —
                    Love,
                        Mom and Dad

I Can't Accept Not Trying

I Can't Accept Not Trying

Michael Jordan on the Pursuit of Excellence

Text by Michael Jordan

Edited by Mark Vancil

Design by McMillan Associates

Photographs by Sandro Miller

HarperSanFrancisco
A Division of HarperCollins*Publishers*

Produced by
Rare Air, Ltd.
A Mark Vancil Company

Edited by
Mark Vancil

Design by
McMillan Associates
130 Washington Street
West Dundee, Illinois 60118

Photographs by
Sandro Miller

Special thanks to:
Colleen Dahlberg, George Kohler, Anne McMillan, and John Vieceli

FIRST EDITION

ISBN 0-06-251190-4

94 95 96 97 98 **WOR** 10 9 8 7 6 5 4 3 2 1

This book may be purchased for educational, business, or sales promotion use. For information, please call or write: Special Markets Department, Harper San Francisco, 1160 Battery Street, San Francisco, CA 94111. Telephone: (415) 477-4400.

Dedicated to my close friends and family,
for the inspiration and support I have received from them.
And to my parents, for the love and guidance they have given me
throughout my life. They are my true role models.

c o n t e n t s

"Step by step. I can't see any other way of accomplishing anything."

I always had the ultimate goal of being the best, but I approached everything step by step. That's why I wasn't afraid to go to the University of North Carolina after high school.

Everyone told me I shouldn't go because I wouldn't be able to play at that level. They said I should go to the Air Force Academy because then I would have a job when I finished college. Everyone had a different agenda for me. But I had my own.

I had always set short-term goals. As I look back, each one of those steps or successes led to the next one. When I got cut from the varsity team as a sophomore in high school, I learned something.

I knew I never wanted to feel that bad again. I never wanted to have that taste in my mouth, that hole in my stomach.

So I set a goal of becoming a starter on the varsity. That's what I focused on all summer. When I worked on my game, that's what I thought about. When it happened, I set another goal, a reasonable, manageable goal that I could realistically achieve if I worked hard enough.

Each time I visualized where I wanted to be, what kind of player I wanted to become.

I guess I approached it with the end in mind. I knew exactly where I wanted to go, and I focused on getting there. As I reached those goals, they built on one another. I gained a little confidence every time I came through.

So I had built up the confidence that I could compete at North Carolina. It was all mental for me. I never wrote anything down. I just concentrated on the next step.

I think I could have applied that approach to anything I might have chosen to do. It's no different from the person whose ultimate goal is to become a doctor. If that's your goal and you're getting Cs in biology then the first thing you have to do is get Bs in biology and then As. You have to perfect the first step and then move on to chemistry or physics.

Take those small steps. Otherwise you're opening yourself up to all kinds of frustration. Where would your confidence come from if the only measure of success was becoming a doctor? If you tried as hard as you could and didn't become a doctor, would that mean your whole life was a failure? Of course not.

All those steps are like pieces of a puzzle. They all come together to form a picture.

If it's complete, then you've reached your goal. If not, don't get down on yourself.

If you've done your best, then you will have had some accomplishments along the way. Not everyone is going to get the entire picture. Not everyone is going to be the greatest salesman or the greatest basketball player. But you can still be considered one of the best, and you can still be considered a success.

That's why I've always set short-term goals. Whether it's golf, basketball, business, family life, or even baseball, I set goals—realistic goals—and I focus on them. I ask questions, I read, I listen. I did the same thing in baseball with the Chicago White Sox. I'm not afraid to ask anybody anything if I don't know. Why should I be afraid? I'm trying to get somewhere. Help me, give me direction. Nothing wrong with that.

Step by step, I can't see any other way of accomplishing anything.

Fear is an illusion.

I never looked at the consequences of missing a big shot. Why? Because when you think about the consequences you always think of a negative result.

If I'm going to jump into a pool of water, even though I can't swim, I'm thinking about being able to swim at least enough to survive. I'm not jumping in thinking to myself, "I think I can swim, but maybe I'll drown." If I'm jumping into any situation, I'm thinking I'm going to be successful. I'm not thinking about what happens if I fail.

But I can see how some people get frozen by that fear of failure. They get it from peers or from just thinking about the possibility of a negative result. They might be afraid of looking bad or being embarrassed. That's not good enough for me.

I realized that if I was going to achieve anything in life I had to be aggressive. I had to get out there and go for it. I don't believe you can achieve anything by being passive. I know fear is an obstacle for some people, but it's an illusion to me.

Once I'm in there, I'm not thinking about anything except what I'm trying to accomplish. Any fear is an illusion. You think something is standing in your way, but nothing is really there. What *is* there is an opportunity to do your best and gain some success.

If it turns out my best isn't good enough, then at least I'll never be able to look back and say I was too afraid to try. Maybe I just didn't have it. Maybe I just wasn't good enough. There's nothing wrong with that and nothing to be afraid of either. Failure always made me try harder the next time.

That's why my advice has always been to "think positive" and find fuel in any failure. Sometimes failure actually just gets you closer to where you want to be. If I'm trying to fix a car, every time I try something that doesn't work, I'm getting closer to finding the answer. The greatest inventions in the world had hundreds of failures before the answers were found.

I think fear sometimes comes from a lack of focus or concentration, especially in sports. If I had stood at the free-throw line and thought about 10 million people watching me on the other side of the camera lens, I couldn't have made anything.

So I mentally tried to put myself in a familiar place. I thought about all those times I shot free throws in practice and went through the same motion, the same technique that I had used thousands of times. You forget about the outcome. You know you are doing the right things. So you relax and perform. After that you can't control anything anyway. It's out of your hands, so don't worry about it.

It's no different than making a presentation in the business world or doing a report for school. If you did all the things necessary, then it's out of your hands. Either the clients liked the presentation or they didn't. It's up to the client, the buyer, or the teacher.

I can accept failure. Everyone fails at something. But I can't accept not trying. That's why I wasn't afraid to try baseball. I can't say, "Well, I can't do it because I'm afraid I may not make the team." That's not good enough for me. It doesn't matter if you win as long as you give everything in your heart and work at it 110 percent.

Fear is an illusion.

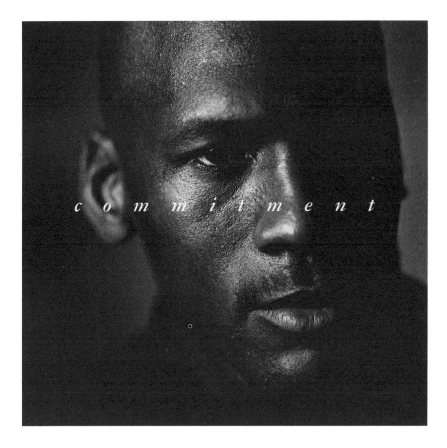

There are no shortcuts.

Coming out of high school, if I had been any less committed or had any less desire to achieve, I would have taken the easy path and gone to another school. But I went to North Carolina because I realized that a lot of Dean Smith's players got drafted by NBA teams. People were telling me I should go around the difficult route, but I wasn't about to do that. I had locked in, committed to my goals. I wanted to find out. I wanted to know where I stood.

I've always believed that if you put in the work, the results will come. I don't do things halfheartedly. Because I know if I do, then I can expect halfhearted results. That's why I approached practices the same way I approached games. You can't turn it on and off like a faucet. I couldn't dog it during practice and then, when I needed that extra push late in the game, expect it to be there.

But that's how a lot of people approach things. And that's why a lot of people fail. They sound like they're committed to being the best they can be. They say all the right things, make all the proper appearances. But when it comes right down to it, they're looking for reasons instead of answers.

You see it all the time in professional sports. You can even see it in your friends or business associates. There are a million excuses for not paying the price. "If I was only given a particular opportunity" or "if only the coach, teacher or boss liked me better, I could have accomplished this or that." Nothing but excuses.

Part of this commitment is taking responsibility. That's not to say there aren't obstacles or distractions. If you're trying to achieve, there will be roadblocks. I've had them; everybody has had them. But obstacles don't have to stop you. If you run into a wall, don't turn around and give up. Figure out how to climb it, go through it, or work around it.

I got a very good lesson about distractions my junior year at North Carolina. My sophomore season turned out to be my best in college.

Because of that, there were all kinds of expectations during my junior year. What I tried to do was come out and live up to those expectations.

I was trying to live up to everyone else's expectations for me instead of following my own road. I found myself standing around looking for the spectacular dunk, cheating out on the defensive end to get that breakaway situation.

Coach Smith called me in one day and showed me two films, one from the beginning of my sophomore season, the other from the beginning of my junior year. They were totally the opposite. I was looking for short-cuts and that wasn't how I got there. I still had the desire, but I had lost my focus.

You have to stick to your plan. A lot of people try to pull you down to their level because they can't achieve certain things. But very few people get anywhere by taking shortcuts. Very few people win the lottery to gain their wealth. It happens, but the odds certainly aren't with them. More people get it the honest way, by setting their goals and committing themselves to achieving those goals.

That's the only way I'd want it anyway.

*Talent wins games, but
teamwork and intelligence
win championships.*

It seems our society tends to glamorize individual levels of success without taking the entire process into consideration. Football is a prime example.

I think football is a backward sport.

Here you have a guy, the quarterback, who is very intelligent and is probably capable of carrying the team. But he can't do that if he doesn't have the protection of the guards and tackles in front of him. Yet those guys make pennies while the quarterback makes nickels. That doesn't make any sense. If you don't have those guys up front, that nickel isn't worth a penny.

It works the same way in a corporation. What if you have a CEO with a great idea, but he doesn't have the people to make it happen? If you don't have all the pieces in place, particularly at the front lines, that idea doesn't mean a thing. You can have the greatest salespeople in the world, but if the people making the product aren't any good, no one will buy it.

On the Bulls, we had two guys with distinct abilities in Bill Cartwright and John Paxson. And we found a way to use those talents within the framework of our team. It's the same with workers on the lower end of the corporate ladder. Managers, just like basketball coaches, have to find a way to utilize those individual talents in the best interests of the company.

When we started winning championships, there was an understanding among all twelve players about what our roles were. We knew our responsibilities and we knew our capabilities.

We knew, for example, that we wanted to go to Bill early and try to get him into the flow of the game. We knew that if John hit his first shot it would open things up for Scottie Pippen, B.J. Armstrong, and myself. Those were the kinds of things we had to understand and accept if we were going to win championships.

It took us a period of time to understand that. It's a selfless process, and in our society sometimes it's hard to come to grips with filling a role instead of trying to be a superstar. There is a tendency to ignore or fail to respect all the parts that make the whole thing possible.

Naturally there are going to be some ups and downs, particularly if you have individuals trying to achieve at a high level. But when we stepped in between the lines, we knew what we were capable of doing. When a pressure situation presented itself, we were plugged into one another as a cohesive unit. That's why we were able to come back so often and win so many close games.

And that's why we were able to beat more talented teams. There are plenty of teams in every sport that have great players and never win titles. Most of the time, those players aren't willing to sacrifice for the greater good of the team. The funny thing is, in the end, their unwillingness to sacrifice only makes individual goals more difficult to achieve.

The one thing I was taught at North Carolina, and one thing that I believe to the fullest, is that if you think and achieve as a team, the individual accolades will take care of themselves.

Me? I'd rather have five guys with less talent who are willing to come together as a team than five guys who consider themselves stars and aren't willing to sacrifice.

Talent wins games, but teamwork and intelligence win championships.

fundamentals

*The minute you get
away from fundamentals,
the bottom can fall out.*

Fundamentals were the most crucial part of my game in the NBA. Everything I did, everything I achieved, can be traced back to the way I approached the fundamentals and how I applied them to my abilities.

They really are the basic building blocks or principles that make everything work. I don't care what you're doing or what you're trying to accomplish; you can't skip fundamentals if you want to be the best. There are plenty of people with great abilities, but if they don't know how to apply those skills to a particular situation, then what good are they? So what if you can jump out of the gym. Can you shoot well enough to score if you're not in position to dunk? So what if you can memorize an entire book for the test. Did you learn anything?

But some guys don't want to deal with that. They're looking for instant gratification, so maybe they skip a few steps. Maybe they don't practice ballhandling because they don't handle the ball that much. Maybe they don't develop proper shooting techniques because they rely on their size to score. You can get away with it through the early stages, but it's going to catch up with you eventually.

It's like they're so focused on composing a masterpiece that they never master the scales. And you can't do one without the other. The minute you get away from fundamentals—whether it's proper technique, work ethic, or mental preparation—the bottom can fall out of your game, your schoolwork, your job, whatever you're doing.

Look at the NBA. You have players with a lot of ability who just can't get over the hump. Why? Because they don't have the fundamentals to build on. They have no foundation. Look at all the big men that were starters in college but end up on the bench in the NBA. Some of them were able to move from level to level by relying on their size or strength. Then they get to the ultimate level and that's not enough. By then it's too late.

When I was at North Carolina, everybody said Dean Smith held me back. They joked about how Coach Smith was the only guy who could hold Michael Jordan under 20 points. But he taught me the game. He taught me the importance of fundamentals and how to apply them to my individual skills. That's what made me a complete player. When I got to the NBA and I had to work on different parts of my game, whether it was shooting or defense, I had that foundation to work from. I knew the way to go about it.

When you understand the building blocks, you begin to see how the entire operation works. And that allows you to operate more intelligently, whether it's in school, business, or even raising a family.

That's what made Larry Bird such a great player. He essentially mastered the fundamentals to the point that he overcame any physical limitations he might have had. It sounds easy, but it isn't. You have to monitor your fundamentals constantly because the only thing that changes will be your attention to them. The fundamentals wil! never change.

It comes down to a very simple saying: There is a right way and a wrong way to do things. You can practice shooting eight hours a day, but if your technique is wrong, then all you become is very good at shooting the wrong way.

Get the fundamentals down and the level of everything you do will rise.

*If you don't back it up
with performance and hard work,
talking doesn't mean a thing.*

I've always tried to lead by example. That is just my personality. I never led vocally. I never really tried to motivate by talking because I don't think words ever mean as much as action.

They always say a picture carries a thousand words. So I tried to paint a picture of hard work and discipline. And I've never stopped. The second I let down, particularly if I'm perceived as the leader of my team or my company, I give others an opening to let down as well. Why not? If the person out front takes a day off or doesn't play hard, why should anyone else?

But a leader has to earn that title. You aren't the leader just because you're the best player on the team, the smartest person in the class, or the most popular. No one can give you that title either. You have to gain the respect of those around you by your actions. You have to be consistent in your approach whether it's basketball practice, a sales meeting, or dealing with your family.

Those around you have to know what to expect. They have to be confident that you'll be there, that your performance will be pretty much the same from game to game, particularly when things get tight.

Ultimately, coaches or players can say anything they want, but if they don't back it up with performance and hard work, the talking doesn't mean a thing. That's why I tried to play through all the little nagging injuries—to make a point, to set a standard. If I was considered the best player or I was making the most money, I wanted everyone to know I earned those things. I wanted everyone around me to understand it wasn't an accident. And I wanted everyone to know I was watching them, too.

A leader can't make any excuses. There has to be quality in everything you do. Off the court, on the court, in the classroom, on the playground, inside the meeting room, outside of work. You have to transfer those skills, that drive, to whatever environment you're in.

And you have to be willing to sacrifice certain individual goals, if necessary, for the good of the team. I think a leader is also a person who has had past successes in certain situations and isn't afraid of taking the chance to lead others down that road again—someone who has a certain vision, almost an ability to look ahead or to anticipate what's coming.

But along the way, you also have to stand up for what you believe and hold on to your convictions. All the people I admire do that. My parents were like that. They never let me down. I knew when the pressure was on they would come through for me. I had confidence in them.

Coach Smith is like that. I think people like Julius Erving, Denzel Washington, Spike Lee, and Martin Luther King—people I admire—all created their own vision. And they didn't let anyone or anything distract them or break them down. They set an example and they led.

But you don't have to be on television, coach an NBA team, or play a professional sport to be an effective leader. Just about every home, every business, every neighborhood and every family needs someone to lead. We've got enough people talking about it.

Harper San Francisco and the author, in association with the Rainforest Action Network, will facilitate the planting of two trees for every one tree used in the manufacturing of this book.

This edition is printed on acid-free paper that meets the American National Standards Institute Z39.48 Standard.